I HAVE A VISION LOSS, AND IT'S OKAY!

Written by
Dr. William M. Bauer

Illustrated by
Mallory Hill

WestBow Press books may be ordered through booksellers or by contacting:

WestBow Press
A Division of Thomas Nelson & Zondervan
1663 Liberty Drive
Bloomington, IN 47403
www.westbowpress.com
844-714-3454

Because of the dynamic nature of the Internet, any web addresses or links contained in this book may have changed since publication and may no longer be valid. The views expressed in this work are solely those of the author and do not necessarily reflect the views of the publisher, and the publisher hereby disclaims any responsibility for them.

Any people depicted in stock imagery provided by Getty Images are models, and such images are being used for illustrative purposes only.
Certain stock imagery © Getty Images.

Interior Image Credit: Mallory Hill

ISBN: 978-1-6642-4730-7 (sc)
ISBN: 978-1-6642-4731-4 (e)

Library of Congress Control Number: 2021912589

Print information available on the last page.

WestBow Press rev. date: 10/19/2021

I HAVE A VISION LOSS, AND IT'S OKAY!

About the Author:

Dr. William M. (Bill) Bauer is a licensed clinical counselor in the rural Mid-Ohio Valley area who was a former classroom teacher, principal, and college professor. He has worked with children and adults with disabilities all of his life and hopes that this book brings an understanding to children with disabilities, their teachers, and their classmates. Dr. Bauer was born with a severe hearing impairment.

THIS BOOK IS DEDICATED TO:

ALL PEOPLE WITH DISABILITIES WHOSE LIVES ARE SHARED IN THIS BOOK SERIES TO MAKE THE WORLD A BETTER PLACE. ALL WE WANT IS TO BE ACCEPTED AS WE ARE, HAVE FRIENDS, LIVE IN OUR COMMUNITIES AND TO DREAM AS OUR NON-DISABLED PEERS.

SPECIAL THANKS TO MY WIFE, MARY ELLA, DAUGHTER MADISON RYSER, HER HUSBAND ANDREW AND GRANDSON JACK.

#GRANTSPEED.
LOVE YOU, SON

Forewords:

I have had the pleasure of working with Dr. Bauer in the professional education and mental health fields for over two decades, and this book series is his latest outstanding work to help young people understand and accept differences. Each title focuses on a uniqueness and assures us that "it is OKAY!"

Dr. Stephanie Starcher
Public School Superintendent

Being different is OK! Every effort to erase stigma surrounding our differences is important. The earlier we start, the better chance we have at preventing stigma from even occurring. I had the honor of meeting Dr. Bill Bauer when I was in college, and it is no surprise his work as a mental health advocate would transpire into this series of books. I'm thankful for his commitment to celebrating our differences.

Nick Gehlfuss, MFA, Actor, film and television.
Currently, Dr. Halstead, Chicago Med.

This book series by Dr. William Bauer — my good friend Bill — fills a niche in children's literature that embraces diversity and self-esteem. This series is not only important, but extremely fun. As founder of Orphans International, I look forward to reading these stories to children of all faiths and abilities around the world. This book is indeed a living testament to Bill's own son. The world is a better place because of Bill Bauer! #GrantSpeed

James Jay Dudley Luce, Founder Orphans International Worldwide,
International Entrepreneur

HI!
MY NAME IS KATHLEEN, AND I AM BLIND.

I BECAME BLIND WHEN I WAS A LITTLE GIRL. IT WAS SCARY, BUT I AM DOING FINE.

SOME PEOPLE CAN SEE EVERYTHING, SOME PEOPLE CAN SEE A FEW THINGS, AND SOME CAN'T SEE ANYTHING.

SOME PEOPLE CAN SEE BUT NOT CLEARLY, THEY HAVE TO GET GLASSES. A VISIT TO THE EYE DOCTOR WILL HELP THEM GET WHAT THEY NEED.

BUT FOR ME, I CAN'T SEE MUCH SO I HAVE SOMEONE WITH ME AT ALL TIMES TO HELP ME MOVE AROUND AND TELL ME WHERE THINGS ARE.

I HAVE A CANE TO MAKE SURE THAT I DON'T BUMP INTO THINGS.

I HAVE TEXT-TO-SPEECH THAT HELPS ME LISTEN TO BOOKS AND ANSWER EMAILS OR TEXT MESSAGES. SOME PEOPLE WHO ARE BLIND READ BY FEELING BUMPS ON PAPER CALLED BRAILLE. IT WAS HARD TO LEARN HOW TO READ IT, BUT I DID IT.

AT SCHOOL, I HAVE AN AIDE WHO HELPS ME GET AROUND AND HELPS ME ORGANIZE FOR MY DAY. MY AIDE AND I ARE VERY CLOSE. I HAVE TO MAKE SURE I TRUST MY AIDE. I COUNT ON HER TO HELP ME.

AT HOME, MY PARENTS ALLOW ME TO BE AS INDEPENDENT AS POSSIBLE. THEY WANT ME TO GROW UP, GET A JOB, AND LIVE ON MY OWN. I WANT THAT TOO.

I GET AROUND THE CITY BY USING PUBLIC TRANSPORTATION OR SOMEONE TAKING ME.

I AM HAPPY WITH WHO I AM, AND I CAN'T WAIT TO SEE WHAT I CAN DO IN THIS WORLD.

MY NAME IS KATHLEEN. I AM BLIND, AND IT'S OKAY!

Printed in the United States
by Baker & Taylor Publisher Services